CW00531693

# THE
# POWER
## OF
# KINDNESS

THE POWER OF KINDNESS

An Hachette UK Company
www.hachette.co.uk

Summersdale Publishers Ltd
Part of Octopus Publishing Group Limited
Carmelite House
50 Victoria Embankment
LONDON
EC4Y 0DZ
UK

www.summersdale.com

Printed and bound in Poland

ISBN: 978-1-78783-818-5

Substantial discounts on bulk quantities of Summersdale books are available to corporations, professional associations and other organisations. For details contact general enquiries: telephone: +44 (0) 1243 771107 or email: enquiries@summersdale.com.

WHEN TIMES ARE HARD
WE PULL TOGETHER

# THE
# POWER
## OF
# KINDNESS

INSPIRING STORIES FROM
THE CORONAVIRUS PANDEMIC

DEBBI MARCO

summersdale

# INTRODUCTION

In 2020, the UK – along with the rest of the world – was hit by the coronavirus crisis. It was an unprecedented time, with thousands of people falling ill across the country. But out of the darkness, pockets of light started to spring up everywhere. A wave of kindness swept the country – and the globe. People from all walks of life went above and beyond to help out neighbours, key workers, NHS staff and even complete strangers. The Red Cross estimates that since the beginning of lockdown, when Brits were asked to stay at home, over 43 million people across the UK did something kind to help others.

So take heart from the uplifting stories, funny lockdown anecdotes and inspiring quotes in this book, from the UK and beyond, all illustrating just how kind people can be – because humankind has proved again and again that, in times of trouble, pulling together is what we do best.

# CLAP FOR CARERS

Annemarie Plas, a Dutchwoman living in South London, wanted to do something to show her appreciation for key workers on the coronavirus front line. Inspired by similar movements in Europe, Annemarie used the power of social media to organise communities across the country to stand on their doorsteps and clap or bang pans at 8 p.m. every Thursday. Not only did this help key workers feel appreciated, but it also brought neighbours closer together. Millions of people around the country showed their support. Even Prince Charles and his wife Camilla joined the nation on several occasions, clapping outside their Scottish home at Birkhall, in Aberdeenshire. A spokesman for the couple said that they wanted to show their continued appreciation for NHS staff and other key workers on the front line. 'The response has been really overwhelming to see,' said Annemarie.

A SINGLE ACT OF

*kindness*

THROWS OUT ROOTS IN
ALL DIRECTIONS, AND THE

*roots spring up*

AND MAKE NEW TREES.

FREDERICK WILLIAM FABER

# BED AND BREAKFAST

The owner of The Flying Horse Hotel, Ben Boothman, from Rochdale, offered free rooms to those who needed to self-isolate, but were unable to stay at home, as they would have endangered their families. His mother needed to self-isolate, so he explained that he wanted to help others in the same situation and spare them unnecessary stress.

# LETTERBOX CHAT

One British postie has gone the extra mile to keep those on his delivery route safe and happy. During the coronavirus crisis, Geoff Sacklyn from Clevedon, North Somerset, knocked on the doors of each of his customers to check they were okay and whether they needed anything. He also took the time to have socially distanced chats with elderly residents to bring them joy. 'It's part of my job to connect with people,' he said. 'Me and my colleague, Steve Twigger, we make the elderly laugh, keep up residents' spirits, get shopping for people and check everyone is okay.'

# KINDNESS IS THE MARK WE LEAVE ON THE WORLD

# Eye-watering onions

Lockdown has meant a lot more screen time for kids. This was certainly the case for one-year-old Alice, who managed to order some onions from Deliveroo when she was playing on her dad's phone. The three-pack only cost £1.50, but by the time the delivery charge was added, they cost an eye-watering £20. Although Dad Jamie cheerfully said he'd make a curry with the costly veg, Deliveroo kindly gave him a gift voucher to cover the cost, when they heard about the mix-up, and even offered to deliver the rest of the ingredients for his meal.

WHEN YOU ARE KIND TO
SOMEONE IN TROUBLE,
YOU HOPE THEY'LL

*remember*

AND BE KIND TO
SOMEONE ELSE. AND
IT'LL BECOME LIKE A

*wildfire.*

WHOOPI GOLDBERG

# CHECKOUT CHARM

Mum-of-four Sophie Gowing realised she had gone over her weekly budget when she got to the till at Morrisons in Aldershot, Surrey. Sophie had overspent because of shortages on the shelves, which had forced her to choose pricier items. As a result, she was £22 short for her shopping. Fighting back tears, Sophie struggled to decide which items to put back, when a man in the queue came up and said that he would pay the balance. A kindly supermarket worker also applied her staff discount to make Sophie's bill even smaller. 'I only have a certain amount of money to spend, which is not a lot. He was lovely. I wanted to get his name, but I was so embarrassed and it all happened so quickly,' she said. The stranger even said Sophie could keep the change, so she had a little bit extra for the rest of the day.

# DRIVE-THROUGH CARE

With many desperate to visit loved ones, a care home in Devon created a drive-through visiting system. Using PPE and carefully coordinated time slots to ensure social distancing, families were able to see residents from the safety of their cars, resulting in plenty of smiles and waving. Definitely better than a burger and fries!

HOW DO WE

*change*

THE WORLD?
ONE ACT OF RANDOM

*kindness*

AT A TIME.

MORGAN FREEMAN

# Dressed to impress

While a small Perthshire town was on lockdown, one good-humoured resident decided to entertain his neighbours from a distance. He dressed up in an inflatable Tyrannosaurus rex costume and roamed the streets, to the delight of the locals. However, some local dogs weren't too impressed, and he set off quite a few barking hounds.

# BE THE REASON SOMEONE BELIEVES IN THE GOODNESS OF PEOPLE

# GIFT LIST

Instead of feeling despondent at home after her wedding was cancelled because of the coronavirus outbreak, Lily Honan, from Corby, started the Random Act of Kindness Northamptonshire Facebook page. Rather than compiling a gift list, as is usual for most brides, she set up the page for strangers to buy a gift for someone else to make them smile. In two weeks, the group grew to over 8,000 members and has continued to spread kindness ever since. One person to benefit from the group was key worker Chelsea McCready from Wellingborough. She was also due to get married and was feeling quite sad, but receiving toys for her two-year-old son Harry made her day. Lily, who usually works as a beautician, dedicated all her time to the Facebook page during lockdown. 'What is the point of sitting around and moping? I would rather see other people smile.'

YOU CANNOT DO A

*kindness*

TOO SOON, FOR YOU
NEVER KNOW HOW
SOON IT WILL BE

*too late.*

RALPH WALDO EMERSON

# HOME SWEET HOME

With jobs at risk during the coronavirus crisis, being able to pay the rent wasn't always going to be straightforward. So when Amy Gledhill's landlord sent her a message promising she would have a roof over her head if her circumstances changed, she nearly cried with relief. Amy then tweeted about the kindness, encouraging others to do the same: 'Landlords, take note. If you're in a position to say this to someone, please do. When we can't rely on the government, we've got to help each other.'

# MAGNETIC ATTRACTION

Determined Daniel Reardon wanted to give the public something that would protect them from the coronavirus. Unfortunately, his efforts landed him in hospital. Just before his admission, the Australian astrophysicist was trying to create a magnetic necklace that would react to facial contact and help to stop the spread of the virus. While experimenting with the magnets, he got some stuck up his nose and then made things worse by trying to remove them with metal pliers. Daniel has now promised he's going to stick to safer projects, like building shelves and tiling.

ASK YOURSELF: HAVE
YOU BEEN KIND TODAY?
MAKE KINDNESS YOUR
MODUS OPERANDI AND

*change your world.*

ANNIE LENNOX

# KINDNESS IS ABOUT DOING ANYTHING YOU CAN, WHEREVER YOU ARE, WITHIN YOUR MEANS

# FLORAL TRIBUTES

When Julie Spence realised lockdown was going to stop her making her annual pilgrimage to lay flowers on the memorial bench of her son Callum, she was heartbroken. On the anniversary of Callum's death, Julie and her family would always visit the cemetery in Leeds, where he was buried, and get the train to Scarborough to go to his memorial bench – a journey she'd made every year for 15 years, since Callum was killed in a road accident when he was eight. Unable to travel, Julie put out an appeal on Facebook. Her request was answered by student Harley Johnson, who not only visited the bench, but also shared Julie's post. As a result, Callum's memorial was covered with flowers brought by strangers.

'It's been overwhelming,' Julie said. 'I can't believe people who don't know me and never knew Callum would do it, especially at times like these. For their help I will be forever grateful.'

# Zoom fail

One boss accidentally turned on the potato filter during a work video-call and was unable to change it for an entire meeting, causing her staff to have fits of giggles. Lizet Ocampo, the national political director of People For the American Way, was holding a weekly Monday morning check-in with her colleagues when she accidentally turned herself into a potato, with only her eyes and mouth visible to her team.

IF I CANNOT DO

*great things,*

I CAN DO

*small things*

IN A GREAT WAY.

MARTIN LUTHER KING

# ALL-STAR DELIVERY

*Game of Thrones* actor Michael Condron switched career paths to become an Asda delivery driver during lockdown. The actor, who played Bowen Marsh in the series, wanted to play an active part in the battle against coronavirus and help those in need to receive their shopping. He said: 'Every single person has a role to play in these times. People now should really appreciate the hard work that everybody does. The job means I can continue to have that interaction with people like I get in a theatre. It's kept me mentally in a good place and it continues to do so.'

# ONE KIND WORD CAN CHANGE SOMEONE'S ENTIRE DAY

# NEIGHBOURLY LOVE

After a house fire left Tracy and Mark Booth homeless and sleeping in a tent, the Essex couple were overwhelmed by the offers of help to rebuild their home from their local community. The Facebook group Colchester Anti-Loo Roll Brigade – which had been set up after the stockpiling of essential goods left people struggling – found them somewhere to live and then put a call out for trades. Within ten minutes they were inundated with people offering them free services, including scaffolding, roofing and electrics. Tracy said: 'I have no words strong enough to say how grateful and how wonderful they have been. I still can't believe the devastation inside and things that have just been totally and utterly destroyed.' She added: 'The people on the Anti-Loo Roll Brigade page have been so amazing. They've kept our spirits up all the time. It's really lovely.'

ALWAYS BE
A LITTLE

*kinder*

THAN

*necessary.*

J. M. BARRIE

# MORE THAN MILK

You may be familiar with milk deliverers leaving a few extras, such as eggs and juice, alongside a pint of the white stuff. But Tony Fowler upped his game during the coronavirus crisis and added lots of different services for his vulnerable customers who had to self-isolate. As well as delivering bread, washing-up liquid and tea to his regulars, the North Leicestershire milkman changed lightbulbs, picked up prescriptions and shared books for his elderly customers. He even took a pet cat to the vet. 'We have had fuel shortages, foot-and-mouth and milk shortages, but I have never let them down before,' he said. 'They trust me to always be there, even in bad weather, to check on them.'

# *Pulling a pint*

Michael Buurman, owner of Hackney's Empress pub, couldn't bear to think of his 90-year-old regular Cyril missing out on his favourite pint when all the pubs closed. So he delivered a barrel of Cyril's favourite ale to his door in East London to ensure he could have a drink whenever he wanted. The thoughtful pub owner even included a box of crisps.

CARRY OUT A

*random act
of kindness...*

SAFE IN THE
KNOWLEDGE THAT
ONE DAY SOMEONE
MIGHT DO THE
SAME FOR YOU.

DIANA, PRINCESS OF WALES

# Lion around

Lions in South Africa's Kruger National Park took advantage of the lack of tourists, since coronavirus prevented visitors going on safari. Ranger Richard Sowry was on patrol when he saw a pride of lions sleeping in the middle of a usually busy road and was able to drive much closer than ever before. 'Lions are used to people in vehicles,' he said. 'If I had walked up, they would never have allowed me to get so close.'

# TWITTER POWER

Samantha Kelly, who has over 50,000 Twitter followers, created the #selfisolationhelp hashtag for anyone in Ireland who needed support or felt lonely. She wrote that she would share their post with her Twitter community, in order to connect them with others in the same situation.

Following on from Samantha's hard work, radio producer Johnathan Randall turned the #selfisolationhelp hashtag into an interactive map, so people could mark themselves as available or find help more easily. The map was a total success, with 3,000 people signing up in 48 hours. Johnathan said: 'What strikes me is that after such a tough week of news, people are made-up to see so much kindness in their region, and people want to be part of it.'

Also inspired by Samantha's example was taxi driver Ray O'Hara, from County Westmeath, who offered to pick up shopping and prescriptions, and drop them at people's doors. 'I just thought about the people [self] isolating and isolated in rural areas, particularly the elderly,' Ray said. 'A lot of them have family that have emigrated overseas and have no one to look out for them.'

# KINDNESS IS CONTAGIOUS – PASS IT AROUND

*Goodness*

IS THE ONLY

*investment*

THAT NEVER FAILS.

HENRY DAVID THOREAU

# FACE-TO-FACE

Throughout the crisis, Facebook groups were created all over the country to connect vulnerable or elderly residents in need of help. More than 200,000 people in the UK became members of more than 300 local support groups set up in the wake of the virus. Rachel Pleasant, from Altrincham in Greater Manchester, recruited volunteers to help local residents who are elderly, vulnerable or stuck at home without any family or friends nearby. She said: 'I think we just felt panic never solves anything. Let's focus some of that energy on really helping the people in our community.'

THREE THINGS
IN HUMAN LIFE
ARE IMPORTANT:
THE FIRST IS TO BE
KIND. THE SECOND
IS TO BE KIND. AND
THE THIRD IS TO

*be kind.*

HENRY JAMES

# PARTY TIME

It's never easy to explain to a six-year-old why they're not having a birthday party, but that is exactly what Tasmin Dawes, from Bury, faced when coronavirus put pay to her son's celebrations. But instead of letting Max's special day fizzle out without a party, Tasmin put out a plea on Facebook, asking children to come over and stick pictures on their window to cheer him up. Thoughtful locals dropped off around 50 cards, pictures and presents for little Max, and the family were blown away by the support. 'People were coming and going all day, people we don't even know,' said Tasmin. 'Kids were even leaving him games to play. It made me feel so happy that everybody cares, it's a good little community. We were smiling all day. Everybody made an effort for a little boy they don't even know.'

# *We will rock you*

Expressing the feelings of many in lockdown, Carlos Díaz Ballesta dressed up like Queen frontman Freddie Mercury and put on a show for his quarantined neighbours from his balcony in Spain. Wearing Mercury's iconic outfit of jeans and white vest, complete with his trademark moustache, the lively Spaniard lip-synced to the Queen hit 'I Want to Break Free', while dancing with a vacuum cleaner, in homage to the song's video.

WHAT YOU DO MAKES
A DIFFERENCE, AND
YOU HAVE TO DECIDE
WHAT KIND OF

*difference*

YOU WANT TO MAKE.

JANE GOODALL

# LOVELY LIPSTICK

Beauty Banks, a charity that supplies essential toiletries to people in poverty, raised £60,000 to pay for soap, hand sanitiser and other items for those without the money to stockpile. Columnist Sali Hughes, who co-founded the campaign, said that because of the coronavirus outbreak people were more able to relate to the idea of struggling to get necessary items. She said: 'I think it's really important in times of crisis, when people are doing something positive it does make you feel a little bit calmer and more in control.'

# 'AISLE DO'

Spare a thought for checkout worker Mandy Hamling who, on the day she was meant to get married, went to work. Although her big day had been cancelled due to the coronavirus pandemic, Mandy's colleagues decorated the Asda store where she worked with balloons and banners as a surprise. She was even presented with a wedding cake and a veil to wear. The store manager announced on the tannoy that it was supposed to be Mandy's special day and played 'Chapel of Love'. All the staff gathered around her to clap and throw confetti, and they even created an umbrella arch for her to walk through. 'It was a really emotional day for me, but they were wonderful,' said Mandy. 'I even had a bunch of flowers given to me from a random customer, which was lovely. The only person that was missing from the day was Michael himself!' Mandy and Michael, her fiancé, rearranged their wedding for 2021.

# KINDNESS IS LOANING YOUR STRENGTH TO SOMEONE INSTEAD OF REMINDING THEM OF THEIR WEAKNESS

# MAKE A MEMORY

The family of Darrell Blackley, who died in hospital after testing positive for coronavirus, were determined his kindly nature would live on. Instead of flowers and cards to mark his passing, they asked people to carry out acts of kindness. 'Help someone who is lonely or struggling during this time, who needs shopping, childcare or a chat. Build something beautiful in Darrell's memory,' his family requested.

# Walk on the wild side

Penguins at Chicago's Shedd Aquarium were given the run of the zoo and began to meet some of their neighbours. The beluga whales were enraptured at the sight of the flightless birds peering into their tanks and swam right up to the glass for a closer look.

# WASH IN ONE

Terry Bourne, a football kitman for Lincoln City FC, turned his laundry skills to helping the overstretched NHS workers during the coronavirus crisis, after seeing the industrial-sized washing machines lying dormant at the club. While the English football season was cancelled, Terry offered to collect washing from Lincoln County Hospital and the local area, aiming to complete 12 loads of washing each day. 'It'll keep me busy,' he said. Football games can only go ahead with NHS volunteers on hand, making it only right that the football club returned the favour when it could.

HOW

*beautiful*

A DAY CAN BE WHEN

*kindness*

TOUCHES IT!

GEORGE ELLISTON

# SCARECROW HOMAGE

Residents of Kilkhampton, a village just outside Bude, put their creativity to the test when it came to giving thanks to key workers. Along with the weekly clap, they created an homage to all those on the front line and built effigies of them. Over 30 scarecrows have been dotted around the village, dressed as police officers, nurses, doctors, posties and paramedics.

# Fancy-dress postie

Postman Jon Matson from Boldon went one step further to keep people amused while delivering their post. Each day he wore a different fancy-dress outfit, transforming into a gladiator, a cheerleader and Little Bo Peep, to name a few. 'When the first person sees me on the round, they start to message their friends, so before I even get there, people are waiting at windows,' said Jon. 'Everybody is laughing and cheering. I even had the police honk their horns at me.'

DON'T JUDGE
EACH DAY BY THE

*harvest*

YOU REAP,
BUT BY THE

*seeds*

YOU PLANT.

ROBERT LOUIS STEVENSON

# CHOCO-KINDNESS

It was only her first month in the job as a papergirl, but 14-year-old Sophie Turner was moved when she saw a note on a pensioner's door that said she was self-isolating. The kind teen posted a Dairy Milk chocolate bar and a note through the letterbox, in an attempt to cheer up the 84-year-old from Darlington.

Sophie explained: 'I saw the sign on the door saying the lady had underlying medical conditions and was self-isolating, and I thought it was sad and would be nice to try and cheer her up with chocolate. I thought it would be good for her to know someone was thinking of her.'

The papergirl later learned that the pensioner, who had recently been widowed and was grieving for her late husband, was very touched by the her act of kindness.

# THERE IS SO MUCH TO GAIN FROM THE ACT OF GIVING

# FEEDING FAMILIES

Head teacher Samantha Ray, from Newcastle-Under-Lyme, knew that some local families would be struggling to make ends meet during lockdown and was concerned about students going hungry. In order to help out, she asked her local pub to make Sunday roast dinners for 30 of them. Then she and her husband delivered the hot meals personally.

# THE POINT IS NOT TO

*pay back*

# KINDNESS, BUT TO

*pass it on.*

JULIA ALVAREZ

# Wedding belles

When a friend of photographer Elyssa Seibel mentioned she wanted a 'fancy wine night' – and sent a picture of herself in her wedding dress to her group chat – an idea sparked. Elyssa decided to get more people involved and organised a socially distanced wedding-dress photo shoot with as many of her neighbours as possible. Soon her street was full of women in their wedding dresses, dancing, riding scooters, drinking champagne and relaxing on chairs outside their homes.

# GOAL!

Marcus Rashford might be a top earning footballer, but he hasn't forgotten his roots. He threw his weight behind children's charity FareShare, which distributes food to children who would otherwise go without free school meals due to closures through lockdown. Not only did his support lead to a huge increase in donations – the charity recorded £20 million in food and financial donations – but his campaign on Twitter also contributed to the government making a U-turn on their policy to provide school meals during the summer holidays. After his campaign success, the England striker tweeted: 'Just look at what we can do when we come together, THIS is England in 2020.'

# NO MATTER WHAT PEOPLE TELL YOU,

## *words and ideas*

# CAN CHANGE

## *the world.*

ROBIN WILLIAMS

# Teddy bears' picnic

Two stuffed bears, Ted and Ed, brought smiles to Stockport locals by acting out scenes of everyday life under lockdown. They could be found camping, mowing the lawn and even relaxing with a spa day. The Moor Bears started up their very own Instagram and Facebook pages to keep everyone updated with their antics during the pandemic. 'Both Ted and Ed were adopted from Costco after we found them causing a mess on the marmalade aisle and they have been living with us ever since,' said their owners.

# WAVE THE FLAG

A teaching assistant spent lockdown putting up small fabric flags inscribed with messages of kindness. Julian Wood started the project in 2018, but it grew during the coronavirus crisis as a way of helping people to cope with the pandemic. Each day he made around 50 flags and cycled around Bristol to put them in parks and streets. He said: 'I've recently put flags around the city that say silly things like "You have got cute elbows" and people loved it. Be kind to yourselves. Everyone is finding it difficult.'

# BE KIND TO UNKIND PEOPLE – THEY NEED IT THE MOST

# DIETING BUS DRIVER

When Carl Harding was furloughed because his obesity put him in a high-risk category, he felt a sense of shame and disappointment that he couldn't work alongside his colleagues. The bus driver from Norfolk decided to take immediate action to ensure he could get back to work during the coronavirus crisis. He went on a strict diet and lost 36 kilograms. Before the crisis Carl had high blood pressure and was physically unfit, but now he is much healthier.

'I had let my diet spiral out of control and there's no denying that I was eating well over 8,000 calories per day,' he said. 'But when I was furloughed, I realised it was now or never. I needed to get back to the job I loved to help my colleagues on the front line.'

BE THOUGHTFUL.
RESPECTFUL.
COMPASSIONATE.

Human.

MILEY CYRUS

# Singing doctor

One former doctor delighted people in his hospital by singing opera. Dr Alex Aldren had previously left medicine to become a professional musician, but the tenor returned to the NHS to help during the coronavirus crisis and used his singing talents to lift the spirits of patients and colleagues at the Royal London and Newham Hospital.

# KINDNESS IS BEING SOMEONE WHO MAKES EVERYONE FEEL LIKE A SOMEBODY

# 24-HOUR SERVICE

The owner of Hunger Hangout, a restaurant in Leadgate, worked around the clock to feed over 160 vulnerable people a day during the pandemic. Anthony Wright paid for food out of his own pocket and, along with his team, was spotted working until the early hours to prepare Sunday lunches for those in need.

DOING *nothing* FOR OTHERS IS THE *undoing* OF OURSELVES.

HORACE MANN

# DESIGNER STYLE

With four relatives working on the coronavirus front line, it was no surprise that 11-year-old Emma Harris wanted to do something to help. Emma, from South-east London, decided to raise money for the NHS with her own clothing line, so she designed a charity T-shirt and tote bag. The enterprising schoolgirl also planned a range of lockdown birthday T-shirts for her school friends and raised a total of over £200 for NHS charities. Emma said: 'When we go out for a run, we count the rainbows in the windows of the houses around us. It is incredible to see everyone coming together to thank the NHS and essential workers who are keeping us safe.' Two of Emma's uncles and two aunts work for the NHS in London hospitals.

# It's for you...

Keepers at Tokyo's Sumida Aquarium were worried their garden eels had started to forget about humans, as they were no longer getting hundreds of visitors. Whenever the keepers walked past, the eels would bury themselves in the sand. Finding it difficult to run routine health checks on these creatures while underground, staff sought the public's help, asking people to make video calls to the eels so they could readjust to human contact again.

# PUMP IT UP

Personal trainer Flo Dowler, from Fulham
in West London, kept her neighbours fit
in lockdown by providing daily workouts
– from the top of a steel container in
her street. She would stand on top of it
and blast out energising 80s music to
help encourage her neighbours to join
in the free 30-minute exercise sessions.

# CARE PACKAGES

A retired carer from Lancashire put her money where her heart was and created care packages for vulnerable people in her area. Sarah Jay spent over £200 on essentials, while neighbours and friends donated further money and food to support her. A local shop ordered the stock on her behalf and paid the VAT on it. Each parcel Sarah made was bespoke and would include anything from pet food to diabetes-friendly products. Sarah also sanitised the items to ensure they were safe, before she delivered them to the homes of nominated elderly residents. 'It can be frightening for people, so I just want to help,' she said. 'I want to do something positive and it's not just about a tin of soup – it is about making a personal connection and supporting them if I can.'

IT TAKES COURAGE
FOR PEOPLE TO
LISTEN TO THEIR OWN
GOODNESS AND

PABLO CASALS

# NEVER GET TIRED OF DOING LITTLE THINGS FOR OTHERS

# Super snacks

For any parent or carer who looked after youngsters in lockdown, the never-ending requests for snacks may sound familiar. But nurse Sarah Balsdon from Northumberland came up with an ingenious idea to meet her children's constant demands: she bought a second-hand vending machine and filled it with snacks. Her children had to do chores around the house or complete homework to earn money to buy a treat. To make it fair, Sarah and her husband also stumped up the cash whenever they treated themselves to a packet of crisps or chocolate bar.

# SUPERMARKET SERVICE

Professional runner Rebecca Mehra came to the aid of an elderly couple she met in a supermarket car park. The pensioners were sitting in their car, too scared to enter the supermarket, as the elderly and vulnerable had been instructed to stay at home during the coronavirus outbreak. They were in tears when they finally beckoned Rebecca over. Hearing their distress, she took their shopping list and completed their shop for them.

# IN THESE MOMENTS, YOU REMEMBER WHAT'S REALLY *important.*

HEIDI KLUM, DURING THE
CORONAVIRUS CRISIS

# FREE SUNDAY LUNCH

The Freemasons in South-east Northumberland were keen to make sure local vulnerable people weren't missing out on their weekly roast, so they set up a system to cook and deliver Sunday lunches. And they kept up the service for over three months. Paul Dunning and Jim Grant, who organised the free food, said: 'During these uncertain times, social distancing begins to affect households, leading to new challenges for everyone, making life even harder and with less contact than ever before. Although we all appreciate the difficult times we are experiencing at the moment, we often forget that others may not be coping as well as we are ourselves.' They added that the project owed its success to the enthusiasm and support of the volunteers, who all helped out.

# Flight of the flamingo

One flamingo at Dudley Zoo didn't abide by the government's 'Stay Safe, Stay Home' message and decided to take its exercise in the form of a stroll round the local neighbourhood. Zookeepers believe a strong gust of wind helped the flamingo on its adventure, but reported it was quickly back home in its enclosure and enjoying breakfast.

# THERE'S A FUTURE FOR EVERYONE AND THERE'S ROOM FOR

## *expansion*

# IN KINDNESS THROUGHOUT.

CAPTAIN TOM MOORE

# GIFT FROM BANKSY

Staff at Southampton General Hospital were thrilled when a gift from graffiti artist Banksy appeared on their walls. It features a boy playing with a nurse action figure, having cast aside his Spiderman and Batman figures. A note accompanying the work read: 'Thanks for all you're doing. I hope this brightens the place up a bit, even if it's only black and white.'

# LOVE DOCTORS

Emergency nurse Jann Tipping and doctor Annalan Navaratnam had to cancel their wedding plans due to the coronavirus crisis, but rather than postponing the event, they decided to get married anyway, while still adhering to the social-distancing rules. They took advantage of the on-site facilities at St Thomas' Hospital in London, where they work, and were kindly granted special permission to get married at the hospital chaplaincy. The service was organised in such a rush that Jann barely had time to get her dress and buy the rings. After the ceremony, they hosted a virtual reception, complete with a first dance and speeches, having sent champagne to their guests' homes in advance. Jann said: 'We wanted to have the ceremony while everyone was still healthy, even if it meant our loved ones having to watch us on a screen. The chaplaincy team worked hard to get permission for us to be married, which we appreciated greatly at a time when so much was going on.'

# CHANGE THE WORLD, ONE ACT OF KINDNESS AT A TIME

# Emergency face masks

After standing in a long queue for the post office, a woman in Kiev was told she would not be served unless she was wearing a mask. The ingenious customer, who didn't have a mask to hand, was reluctant to rejoin the back of the queue, so she whipped off her knickers and put them around her face instead.

TAKE CARE OF
YOUR BODIES AND
HEARTS. AND LEAVE

*room for joy.*

RYAN REYNOLDS

# PUPPY LOVE

Music teacher Chris Hannah knew his students would be missing the visits from his pet, Cole, a certified therapy dog, who was a regular in Mennies Elementary School and around the community. So Chris drove Cole past all the children's houses to make sure they wouldn't miss his canine grin and wagging tail. The children were thrilled and decorated their driveways with posters to welcome their puppy pal.

A KIND AND

*compassionate*

ACT IS OFTEN ITS

*own reward.*

WILLIAM JOHN BENNETT

# CARING CALLS

Instead of letting their patients suffer alone, cancer support workers and therapists swapped face-to-face meetings for weekly kindness calls. Staff at the Trinity Holistic Centre, based in Middlesbrough, made the change during the coronavirus lockdown. The centre usually provides emotional support, advice, counselling and complementary therapies, but due to being classed as a high-risk group, the cancer patients couldn't access any of the much-needed on-site services. Volunteer Maxine Nicholson said: 'Despite the fact we've lost all our usual income we didn't want to furlough the staff because we wanted to launch this new service. Without these calls some of the patients might suffer emotionally, with nobody to talk to.'

# BE KIND – THERE ARE PEOPLE AROUND YOU FIGHTING BATTLES YOU KNOW NOTHING ABOUT

# Lunch in a bucket

A kind-hearted couple who delivered lunch to a customer diagnosed with terminal cancer created an ingenious way to get him his meals without breaking social-distancing rules. Sandwich-shop owner Jan Harding and her husband, Barry, would visit John Goodfellow's home and wait for him to lower a bucket from his upstairs window, in which they placed his food, before he pulled it up again.

# HOW WE APPROACH EACH OTHER AND OUR COMMUNITIES WITH

## *empathy and kindness*

# IS INDISPUTABLY IMPORTANT RIGHT NOW.

HARRY AND MEGHAN,
THE DUKE AND DUCHESS OF SUSSEX

# PRINT-TASTIC

The lack of suitable PPE for healthcare workers had been in the news since early on during the coronavirus outbreak. Jo Newman knew that Design and Technology teachers across the UK were starting to make protective visors for key workers, so she inspired her department to do the same.

The Weald Community School had two laser cutters and materials readily available for making masks. Together with her colleagues Nigel Hobbs and Richard Stevens, and a couple of keen students, Jo started to manufacture the protective gear. When they ran out of materials, the local community of Billingshurst donated funds which enabled them to buy more plastic and keep going.

The school made over 700 masks which were donated to care homes, the ambulance service, doctors' surgeries, hospitals and pharmacies. Across the UK, over 400 Design Technology departments in schools were involved in making face masks to help protect key workers.

# Llama calling

Elderly residents in Pembrokeshire, Wales, were treated to a special delivery when a local couple decided to use their llamas to transport essentials. Matt Yorke and his fiancée, Alex, found their animals were the perfect solution to negotiating the bumpy roads, as well as brightening up people's days.

# TO BE KIND IS TO

*be alive.*

ABHIJIT NASKAR

# SHORT SHRIFT

When hairdresser Amanda Glen from Wallsend, in North-east England, heard that The Children's Society charity was struggling with funds because of coronavirus, she wanted to help. She decided it was only fitting to raise money by shaving her head and smashed her initial target of £100. 'I thought I'd do something to help. I've been overwhelmed by the response,' said Amanda, who raised over £600.

# A SINGLE

## *kind word*

# KEEPS ONE WARM FOR

## *three winters.*

### CHINESE PROVERB

# NEVER LOOK DOWN ON SOMEONE UNLESS YOU ARE HELPING THEM UP

# TIME TO HELP

Many people went above and beyond in the time of the coronavirus crisis, and Maggie Martin, from Cramlington, was one such person. She was even crowned a community champion by her local MP for her charity throughout the lockdown. Maggie organised over 100 volunteers to deliver food parcels to vulnerable people and carry out gardening tasks for those who were self-isolating, all the while looking after her autistic son and working. 'It is lovely to receive the award and I was almost speechless when I was told, which is really not like me,' said Maggie. 'I have just tried to do whatever I can to help and there have been so many people in community groups that have also been involved.'

# Fairy masks

As she watched her mum, Kayla, sewing
face masks for key workers, seven-year-old
Evolette from Michigan asked her to make a
special one. After losing her tooth, Evolette
insisted that the tooth fairy should be provided
with a tiny face mask for protection, too.
Her mum obliged, and the tooth fairy left a
note thanking the pair for their kindness.

# LONG-DISTANCE FAN

After spotting pensioner Eva Bowers
waving her thanks to lorry drivers on
the bridge over the M180 in North
Lincolnshire during her permitted
quarantine walk, long-distance driver
David Crossley used social media to
track down his super-fan. He then
sent her flowers and chocolates
to thank her for her support.

# YOU CANNOT BREAK THE

*human spirit.*

KATY PERRY

# TRUE
# KINDNESS
# EXPECTS
# NOTHING IN
# RETURN

# POSTERS OF LOVE

A foster mum from Swansea spent her time in lockdown trying to spread happiness and hope by putting up posters. Lisa Merrett created over 40 rainbow posters, complete with inspirational quotes. She laminated them and tied them to lamp posts all around the local area to give strength and positivity to people who were out on their daily walk. Lisa said: 'This is a very tough time for all of us at the moment, but it is important to keep occupied and keep positive. Every day we do different activities that are fun and new. It is helping us get through these challenging times.'

# Bring back the bacon

Without the ability to round up a search party in lockdown, the owners of a missing sausage dog had to use a specialist trick to locate their missing puppy, Floyd. The seven-month-old miniature dachshund had been missing for three days on the 350-acre farm in Middleton Tyas, North Yorkshire, so on the advice of a specialist dog tracker, owners Fern Holmes and Doug Dinwiddie used the smell of frying bacon to entice the roaming puppy home – and it worked!

# ONLINE STORY TIME

After the libraries closed, one mum took it upon herself to replace the vital storytelling service her local library in Swindon offered to little ones. Lisa Shearing, along with her two children – Jack, nine, and Billy, five – hosted a 15-minute virtual storytelling session on the Liden Library Facebook page, which was viewed thousands of times.

REMEMBER THERE'S
NO SUCH THING AS A

*small act*

OF KINDNESS.
EVERY ACT CREATES
A RIPPLE WITH

*no logical end.*

SCOTT ADAMS

# FIRST-CLASS FLYER

It was an unhappy time when Sheryl Pardo made the decision to fly from Washington DC to Boston to say goodbye to her 83-year-old mother Sandra Wilkins, who was in hospice care.

Pardo was nervous about having to fly during the coronavirus pandemic, but decided she had no choice but to be by her mother's side. As she was the only passenger on the flight, she was allowed to sit in first class and all announcements were personalised to her throughout the journey. Even the captain got in on the fun, giving Pardo a personal shout-out as well. 'Welcome, Sheryl, to 10,000 feet,' he said, after the plane reached a cruising altitude.

Air stewardess Jessica tried to make Sheryl's journey fun despite her tough situation, telling her: 'We'll pretend this is your charter plane, your private jet, you're VIP.' And she added, 'We're making light of the situation, because that's all you can do.'

# Boogie break

Workers on the Worcestershire Acute Hospitals NHS Trust maternity ward shook off their stresses by having a boogie. They boosted the spirits of patients and staff by lip-syncing and dancing along to disco favourite 'We Are Family' by Sister Sledge. In a tweet from the NHS Trust, it was assured the dancers all kept two metres apart.

# HOME GOAL

Football pundit Gary Neville offered rooms in his two hotels to NHS workers and medical professionals to allow them to self-isolate from family members while they worked on the front line. Gary said: 'We've been in consultation with health services and our 176 beds will be occupied by National Health Service workers and medical professionals. They will be free of charge, our staff will operate the hotels as normal and the health workers will be able to stay there without any cost.'

# *Kindness*

## IS JUST

### *love*

## WITH WORK
## BOOTS ON.

ANNA FARIS

# BE KIND TO YOURSELF AS WELL AS TO OTHERS

# TOP OF THE CLASS

Kindly teachers from Brighton Hill Community School in Basingstoke pledged their overtime wages to feed local NHS workers. The teachers donated over £900 to provide meals for staff at Basingstoke and North Hampshire Hospital. And to increase the kindness, the 15 teachers behind the initiative used a struggling local catering firm to provide the food. Head teacher Chris Edwards said it was good to have a little circle of positivity in such difficult times and that he and his team didn't feel comfortable accepting extra government payments for working during the Easter holidays to support children of key workers. 'It's a privilege to be able to do something like this,' he said. 'I hope it's well received in the way it's intended. We're happy to help in any way we can.'

# Fancy a drink?

Portland resident Nicole Hudson was applauding
local healthcare workers when she started chatting
to her upstairs neighbour Phillip Kirkland, as they
both leaned out of their windows. Keen to keep
things social, he offered to share his wine, but in
order to get around the social-distancing restrictions,
he had to pour her measure from his window,
which Nicole then had to catch in her glass.

# BURPEE BENEFITS

After he was furloughed, John Leach
of Houghton-le-Spring set himself a
challenge to collect as much PPE as
possible in 24 hours. He then promised
to do a burpee for each pound he raised
and soon found himself exhausted
but with £800 of donations. He spent
the money creating care packages
for carers, including gloves, masks,
aprons and other essential items.

MOMENTS LIKE THESE
CAN BE INCREDIBLY

*introspective*

AND REFLECTIVE. THEY...
MAKE US MORE FULL,

*compassionate*

AND MINDFUL PEOPLE.

NAOMI CAMPBELL ON THE
CORONAVIRUS PANDEMIC

# SPECIAL DELIVERY

A nurse from Maidenhead, Berkshire, doubled up her shifts to ensure that life-saving stem cells could be delivered to blood cancer patients who desperately needed them to survive. Hayley Leonard volunteered to be a courier alongside her day job as a lead nurse at blood cancer charity Anthony Nolan. Her voluntary role involved travelling across the UK, collecting donated stem cells and delivering them to patients waiting for a transplant. Henny Braund, chief executive of Anthony Nolan, said: 'The reason we've been able to take swift and immediate action to ensure lives can be saved is because of our wonderful team, like Hayley. Our team is working around the clock to keep stem cell donations moving during this difficult period, to save patients' lives.'

# POP-UP BAR

Isolation and a change of routine are
very troubling for people who live with
autism, which is why Gemma Hadley
and her team at Autism Wessex built a
pub in the back garden of a care home.
It was designed for one of their residents
whose routine was to visit his local pub
every day for a Coca-Cola and crisps.

# X-ray vision

A Russian nurse's attempt to keep cool resulted
in a telling-off when she took off her uniform.
She was wearing her PPE gown over the top
but did not realise how transparent it was. The
20-year-old was working on the ward when bosses
informed her that her underwear was in full view.

TRY TO BE A

*rainbow*

IN SOMEONE'S
CLOUD.

MAYA ANGELOU

# BOOK CLUB

English teacher Sam Draper offered a book-club service for over-70s in isolation. He provided them with a phone consultation to discuss what they read, as well as their likes and dislikes, and then sent them books based on their tastes. Once they finished a book, they would have a follow-up conversation to talk through the story and how they found it. Sam, from London, said: 'There's nothing better than sharing a book that you have loved with someone else who loves books. I thought this might provide a brighter moment for people who are stuck at home on their own during these times, when everything feels quite bleak. Hopefully, it's something people can look forward to and help while away the time a little.'

# *Beat this*

Welsh BBC weatherman Owain Wyn Evans gave bosses a surprise after they suggested he try working from home. The TV favourite made headlines when he finished his daily weather forecast by playing along to the BBC news theme tune on the drums. 'When they said try working from home, I didn't realise they'd expect me to do the music too,' he said.

# KINDNESS IS DOING ORDINARY THINGS WITH EXTRAORDINARY LOVE

# RUN FOR FUN

After hearing how hard the Newcastle Dog & Cat Shelter was hit by the coronavirus outbreak, 11-year-old Autumn wanted to help. As a member of the Newcastle Swim Team, she could not do her usual training so instead she decided to run five kilometres with her mum every day to keep fit and raise vital funds for her favourite charity. Autumn set up a fundraising page and, despite hating running, stuck to her goal and made over £1,500.

# Kindness

## IS THE

## *noblest*

## WEAPON.

THOMAS FULLER

# TRUE ROMANCE

Lockdown couldn't stop true love, as Bob Shellard, 90, proved on his sixty-seventh wedding anniversary. Although, due to the coronavirus pandemic, he couldn't visit his wife Nancy, 88, at her nursing home in Stafford Springs, Connecticut, he made a sign and stood outside her window with a huge bunch of balloons. Bob's sign read: 'I've loved you sixty-seven years and still do. Happy anniversary.' Their daughter, Laura Mikolajczak, said she hoped this would show people that they still have to live their life during times of crisis: 'Even with all of this uncertainty and fear going on with the coronavirus, it's important to continue to express your love and continue tradition.'

WE NEED TO

*stick together*

AND LOOK OUT FOR
EACH OTHER DURING
THIS CRAZY TIME.

JUSTIN TIMBERLAKE ON THE
CORONAVIRUS PANDEMIC

# Un-seasonal cheer

The Marsh family broke all the rules of Christmas to cheer up their local community. Instead of waiting until December to switch on their festive lights, Claire and Danny, who have two children and live in Corby, dragged their displays out of storage and switched on the ultimate light show. Claire said: 'In a time of doom and gloom we just wanted to make people smile. We always put a lot of Christmas lights up. Everyone knows where our house is.' The lights were spotted by people returning from night shifts, who thanked the family on social media.

# HAPPINESS IN A BOX

Queen of kindness and writer Bernadette Russell made Happy Boxes for the teachers and classes at her local school, Deptford Park Primary, in London. She said the little boxes could be used to keep writing, drawings or objects in. She cut out golden stars for little ones to write wishes on and pop under pillows, while some delicious biscuits also found their way into the packages.

# THE MORE HAPPINESS YOU GIVE, THE MORE YOU GET IN RETURN

# COMFORT BREAK

While PPE shortage was a big problem during the coronavirus crisis, so was wearing such uncomfortable personal protective equipment for those who had to use it every day. Jade Tillson couldn't bear to watch key workers suffer, so she asked her mum to make some headbands and button extensions to stop the kit digging in. It proved so popular she had to ask craft groups across the country to help. Jade, who works for a company which runs adult social services on behalf of Somerset County Council, then distributed the kits to 900 staff who support adults living in their own homes or residential settings across the county. 'People have been amazingly kind,' said Jade. 'Over the past couple of weeks, I have been organising how many are needed in each of our services and driving around collecting headbands for everyone.'

LOVE CREATES A

*communion*

WITH LIFE.
LOVE EXPANDS US,
CONNECTS US,

*sweetens us,*

ENNOBLES US.

JACK KORNFIELD

# Party bears

The animal residents of California's Yosemite National Park took advantage of the lack of visitors and quiet roads during lockdown and roamed freely down the usually car-packed paths. The bears have also been spotted climbing trees close to the rangers' homes. 'For the most part, I think they're having a party,' said ranger Katie Patrick.

ON BEHALF OF FAKE
DOCTORS EVERYWHERE,
WE WANT TO THANK THE
ACTUAL HEALTHCARE

*superheroes*

ON THE FRONT LINES
OF THIS CRISIS.

OLIVIA WILDE ON THE
CORONAVIRUS PANDEMIC

# LOCAL SERVICE

A convenience store near Falkirk, Scotland, gave away face masks, antibacterial hand gel and cleaning wipes for free to elderly customers. The Day-Today Express also offered a free delivery service to those who were self-isolating. The kindness and generosity of owners Asiyah Javed and her husband Jawad made them local heroes, with the gesture costing them over £2,000. 'We are just trying to help people who can't get out the house,' said Asiyah.

# IF YOU CAN
# BE ANYTHING,
# BE KIND

# 'LIVE ON THE DRIVE'

Singer and psychology student Ellie Mae McHenry, from Morpeth in Northumberland, put her skills to the test when she started to perform a song for her neighbours every Thursday after the Clap for Carers. Her performances were so popular and uplifting that she went on to organise a whole concert, 'Live on the Drive', in order to raise money for the NHS. The concert featured an uplifting and eclectic mix of songs from 1935 to the modern day, so she could keep all her neighbours happy, whatever their musical taste. The singer raised over £1,200 for the SHINE Fund. 'I didn't expect to raise so much. I started with a target of £200, so I am blown away. From the bottom of my heart, I thank all who have supported me and who have so kindly donated,' she said.

COMPASSION
ISN'T ABOUT

*solutions.*

IT'S ABOUT GIVING ALL

*the love*

THAT YOU'VE GOT.

CHERYL STRAYED

## Super dad

One father went the extra mile to ensure his daughter
didn't miss out during lockdown. Mia Finney shared
on her TikTok account how her dad dressed up
as a theatre attendant to serve her popcorn and
check her ticket to recreate a cinema trip. The
fully committed dad also created a drive-through
Starbucks using household items such as a Wii steering
wheel, a NutriBullet blender and printed logos.

# KINDNESS IS A

## *language*

## WHICH THE DEAF
## CAN HEAR AND THE

## *blind can see.*

ANONYMOUS

# MEALS ON WHEELS

Mio Vidakovic, a research associate at City, University of London, cooked and delivered fresh, healthy food to NHS hospitals. His initiative, which he named Furloughed Foodies, began when he noticed that canteens in most hospitals shut at 5 p.m. and those who worked in the COVID-19 wards weren't allowed in other areas of the hospital. It meant staff struggled when it came to evening meals. Furloughed Foodies soon had around 200 volunteers to cook and deliver food to the hospitals at allocated time slots throughout the crisis.

# KINDNESS IS A GIFT EVERYONE CAN AFFORD TO GIVE

# RENT-FREE

Landlords often get a bad rap but Mario Salerno, the owner of 18 apartment buildings in New York, was adamant he didn't want tenants to stress about money during the coronavirus pandemic. When some of his tenants told him they were worried about paying their rent because they had lost their jobs due to the pandemic, he cancelled all payments for the month of April, costing him thousands of dollars. 'My concern is everyone's health,' he said. 'I told them just to look out for your neighbour and make sure that everyone has food on their table.'

One of his tenants said she's been out of work since she was ordered to shut down her hair salon. 'He's a wonderful man,' said Kaitlyn Guteski. 'It's a game-changer.'

141

HOW CAN THERE
BE MORE MEANING
THAN HELPING
ONE ANOTHER

*stand up*

IN A WIND AND
STAY WARM?

ANNE LAMOTT

# CELEBRATING CARERS

While people in the UK stood on their doorstep every Thursday at 8 p.m. to acknowledge the hard work of NHS and key workers, one Welsh family took it a stage further. Whenever NHS nurse Lynne Lakes returned home, her children found different ways to surprise her as she walked in the door. Her husband Richard, sons Jon and Peter, daughter Zoe, and Zoe's fiancé, Joshua, surprised her each day with applause, confetti, flowers and even by blasting out Tina Turner's 'Simply the Best', along with enthusiastic clapping. 'She's just the most selfless person anyone knows,' said Peter. 'We are extremely proud of her. Our mum works so hard, not only at work, but in every area of her life. She has even made jams to give out to the locals to raise the spirits of our street. She is truly amazing and deserves every single clap she gets.'

# Bin-day fun

People in Australia made the most of the lockdown by dressing up to take out their bins. Aussies have worn everything from inflatable T-rex fancy-dress costumes to their best formal gowns. The Facebook group Bin Isolation Outing, where people could post pictures of their fancy dress, grew to over 1 million members.

# BIRTHDAY TREATS

When centenarian Betty Gutteridge
from Warwickshire had to cancel her
one-hundredth birthday celebrations
due to the coronavirus lockdown, local
firefighters stepped in to help. The
Warwickshire Fire and Rescue Service
set up a special socially distanced
surprise to help her mark the day,
attended by the fire crew themselves
and members of the local community.

# LET'S MAKE KINDNESS THE NEW NORMAL

# PRINCESS OF KINDNESS

With birthday parties cancelled across the UK, professional princess Charlotte Bredael, from Newcastle, was determined to put a smile on children's faces, if she could. Charlotte, who works as an entertainer for children's parties and events where she dresses up as various princesses, saw many Facebook posts about cancelled trips to Disneyland and spoiled birthdays, and that spurred her into action. Charlotte created over 20 videos from her home, dressed as Disney princesses, for any child who was feeling down. 'I thought that if the kids weren't able to meet a princess at Disney World, it might make it a little bit better for them if they could have a video from a princess,' she said. 'It's making the kids really happy and it's also making the parents happy to see their kids happy.'

# BE KIND,

## *be respectful,*

# BE AWARE.

BELLA HADID

# EMERGENCY SHOP

Ambulance worker Hayley Hylands nearly cried when, after an exhausting ten-hour shift, a kindly stranger paid for her weekly shop in Tesco. The key worker had grabbed her purse to pay for her shopping at the checkout when a man appeared and asked her to step back. As she moved away, the stranger took out his card and paid for over £50 worth of shopping. He even threw in a giant Easter egg for Hayley to enjoy, after he spotted she'd bought her children a chocolate treat. 'No one has ever made me feel like that and it is so encouraging to be noticed by a stranger,' said Hayley. 'I was so shaken I didn't even get his name and I would love to reach out to him now and thank him.'

# Table for two

While most people find squirrels stealing nuts from their birdfeeders a pain, Rick Kalinowski felt the opposite and wanted to encourage the furry nut-eaters. After losing his job in the coronavirus pandemic, he decided to use his spare time to build tiny wooden picnic benches for squirrels, which he attached to walls and fences in his garden. They were so popular that he opened an Etsy store and received over 400 orders in the first 24 hours.

*Talk less*

OUT OF HATE,
MORE OUT OF

*empathy.*

JEREMY LIN

# AYE AYE, CAPTAIN

Passengers quarantining for two weeks on the *Diamond Princess* cruise ship praised their captain Gennaro Arma, who waited until all of them had left the vessel before he disembarked. He also did his best to keep in good spirits, sharing informative announcements and maintaining a sense of humour. 'Captain Arma was courageous, sympathetic and carried himself with dignity and optimism for what was an unprecedented and unique situation,' said Aun Na Tan, a passenger from the ship.

# KINDNESS
# MEANS BUILDING
# BRIDGES INSTEAD
# OF WALLS

# FIVE-STAR SERVICE

Supermarket manager Richard Allen, from Cornwall, couldn't stop himself from getting involved when he saw an elderly customer only buying tinned food during lockdown. Taking matters into his own hands, he asked if he could get her any fresh food. When she explained that she had no oven or microwave and no family living locally to provide her with hot meals, Richard arranged for a local café to deliver to her regularly. He even went to her home, so he could fix her broken doorbell. The local café, Miss Molly's, was already offering a discounted 'meals on wheels' service to the vulnerable, but when Richard offered to settle the bill personally, they refused. Leander Connaughton, who works at Miss Molly's, later posted online: 'This is a shout-out to Richard, manager at Aldi Camborne, who noticed a customer in need two weeks ago and stepped up to help out. You, sir, are bl**dy amazing.'

## Panda pals

A restaurant in Thailand came up with a clever way to ensure its customers socially distanced when they came to eat. Staff sat giant toy pandas in seats, carefully positioning them to help diners to keep a distance without feeling awkward. Plus, this made sure everyone had a dining buddy.

# RUBBISH PRESENTS

Teenager Keiahna Jackson from Yarm, North Yorkshire, had been celebrating her eighteenth birthday when her family realised that the envelope containing the £450 she'd been gifted in cash had been discarded along with the wrapping paper. Her mum, Leanne Best, called the council and they sprang into action, with the refuse collection crew wading through the piles of rubbish they had picked up that day. Leanne said: 'In the current climate I was really mindful that money is tight for people. I was thinking: how do I tell all those people that sent her gifts in the post?' But the refuse collectors found the envelope and even drove back to her home to drop off the cash that same day. They were treated to applause from the neighbours on the street and Leanne said she had no words to express the gratitude she felt.

# WORKOUT HERO

Celebrity personal trainer Joe Wicks put himself on the world stage during lockdown by offering to be the nation's PE teacher. As school was cancelled, Joe launched his 'PE with Joe' service that aired every weekday at 9 a.m. Families members around the country, both young and old, started to lunge, squat and jog in front of their TV sets. As well as helping everyone stay fit, and gaining nearly 1 million viewers for one class, Joe earned himself a place in the Guinness World Records. He also donated his advertising profits, which added up to over £91,000, straight to the NHS. He said: 'So I've decided that as long as I'm the nation's PE teacher, every single penny of the money generated on these videos is going to the place where we need it the most right now. All of it is going straight to the NHS, to support the real heroes right now.' Joe was so committed to keeping his classes going that he even roped in his wife, Rosie, to take the sessions after an operation on his hand left him unable to exercise.

TO BE KIND –
IT COVERS

*everything,*

TO MY MIND.
IF YOU'RE KIND
THAT'S IT.

ROALD DAHL

# Twit-twoo who?

What sounded like pesky pigeons on a Belgian balcony turned out to be a nesting owl, as one resident discovered during lockdown. Jos Baart, who lives in a third-storey apartment, thought the noisy birds were pigeons, but instead it was a Eurasian eagle owl, who went on to give birth to three chicks. They now watch Jos's TV through the window. 'You can see how relaxed they are,' he said. 'They're not scared at all. For me, it's like watching a movie.'

# ON YER BIKE

When Brit Adam Mileusnic found himself
locked down in Madrid, he came up with
an alternative way to get his daily exercise.
He live-streamed an eight-hour cycling
challenge on his bike to raise over £1,000
for the charity Family for Every Child,
which at the time prioritised children
affected by the coronavirus crisis.

# BE GRACIOUS, BE KIND

# FRIENDS FOR LIFE

Friendships can emerge from the strangest of places and two men in particular can vouch for this, as they met while battling coronavirus together. Dave Lewins and Jules Annan fought their way back to health on a ward in Cheltenham Hospital. 'Dave was the only person I saw in the whole time I was there… it was just great to see someone recovering from it,' said Jules.

# Donkey darling

It was an emotional occasion when Ismael Fernandez, from southern Spain, was finally reunited with his beloved donkey, Baldomera, after two months of coronavirus-induced separation. Ismael was prepared for the donkey not to recognise him, but his pet's excited hee-haws soon caused him to break down in tears. The donkey was a gift from his father and the pair are inseparable.

GENTLENESS AND

*kindness*

WILL MAKE OUR HOMES A

*paradise*

ON EARTH.

C. A. BARTOL

# HOME DELIVERY

Keen chef Tom Marsden from Manchester decided to cheer up neighbours by whipping up a home-cooked curry and delivering it to their doorsteps. He spent £150 on ingredients to make a huge batch of chicken curry, with a veg option for those who don't eat meat. It took him two days to make up the 80 portions, which he and his wife, Katy, delivered – complete with naan bread and rice. After leaving the curry on their doorsteps, they sent their neighbours a text, saying, 'You've got a little pressie.' Tom was inspired by a friend who left Prosecco and flowers on his doorstep as a pick-me-up. 'It was just a random act of kindness when everyone's a bit down and gloomy,' he said.

# Handsome hound

For those looking for lockdown fashion inspiration, Hank the Newfoundland, from Wisconsin, did not disappoint. Hank's creative owners dressed him up and styled his fur differently every day, from Joe Exotic to a tarot-card reader, and shared his fashion shoots online. 'He just thinks it's great – it's a head massage,' said Hank's owner, Hannah.

# BLOOMING GREAT

With many people having to work while others were isolating, small gestures really made a difference during the coronavirus crisis. So when shopworker Zoe Hopkins, from Dursley, found a flower bouquet at her work, with a message attached saying 'To all the Boots staff, with love and appreciation', it made her day.

# YOUR CANDLE WILL STAY JUST AS BRIGHT EVEN WHEN YOU SHARE ITS FLAME WITH OTHERS

# SLEEPOVER STAFF

Ten members of staff at a care home in Devon opted to stay in full-time quarantine with their dementia patients to avoid infecting them with coronavirus. The kindly carers at The White House did not return home, or see their own families or children, for over six weeks so they could take care of 17 elderly residents. Staff said they did miss their families, but they formed a close bond with the residents and noticed that the patients were calmer. A spokesperson for the care home said: 'It's incredible what they have done. They decided it was too risky for them to be coming and going. It's a big sacrifice but they came forward themselves and offered to do this. It has paid off – they have not had coronavirus in the home.'

One worker, Sorelle Martin, added: 'My daughter lives with me and we keep in touch... but it's very strange not seeing her... We've all got even closer to the residents. They're like family anyway but they are even more like family now.'

# Sushi train

When you're desperately missing the conveyor belt of food in YO! Sushi because of lockdown, there's only one thing to do: recreate your own at home. And that's exactly what student Chaise Douglas did. Using a Lego train set, he and his roommates made sushi rolls and even colour-coded the plates, before setting the mechanism in motion and grabbing their dinner.

TREAT EVERYONE
WITH POLITENESS
AND KINDNESS, NOT
BECAUSE THEY ARE
NICE, BUT BECAUSE

*you are.*

ROY T. BENNETT

# GET READING

Neighbours in South Ealing, London, created a street library for people to share books safely during the lockdown. Those passing by were encouraged to take a look inside the blue makeshift cabinet, select a book of their choice and drop one off in exchange. To ensure there was never a book shortage, the organisers kept refilling the shelf whenever it got empty.

# FANS TO THE RESCUE

One football fan was so upset to see his favourite team struggling financially that he sent an envelope containing cash to the chairman, Simon Hallett. Kasra Sherrell, a ten-year-old Plymouth Argyle fan who lives in New York, was desperate to help when he saw the chairman's note on the website about the club's financial problems. The Sherrell family have been Argyle supporters for generations, so Kasra didn't think twice before he rounded up all his pocket money, including a £10 note he'd kept from his last trip to England, and put it in an envelope for his dad to post. Supporters all over donated to Plymouth Argyle's fundraiser, smashing its £50,000 target in four days.

# Tiger tales

It seems lockdown may have played with some people's imaginations, since walkers in Kent spotted a tiger roaming free. Armed officers and a police helicopter were despatched to locate the fearsome beast, but on arrival they discovered that the 'tiger' was actually a life-sized sculpture made over 20 years ago by a local artist.

# KINDNESS
# NEVER GOES
# OUT OF STYLE

# REWORKED WEDDING

Canadian couple Anastasija and Josh Davis were supposed to get married in April in front of 135 guests, but quarantine soon put an end to their plans. Instead, the couple got married in Josh's parents' living room in front of immediate family and the best man. When they hopped in a limousine to another location to take photos, their friends surprised them by lining the streets with signs, balloons and streamers, and playing music from their cars. 'They were honking, cheering, yelling congratulations,' Anastasija said. 'Seeing them on the street, celebrating our day with us, made it so magical.'

# PENNE PANIC

Being in lockdown with children is never easy, but it was particularly stressful for Tabatha Stirling from Leith who struggled to find her son's favourite food. Her son, Teddy has Asperger's and a selective eating disorder which means he only eats certain foods. Panic buying meant the shelves emptied of Teddy's favourite penne pasta. The stressed mum put a plea on Twitter offering to trade pasta for homemade shortbread or rice and was soon inundated with offers. She said: 'In a crisis the good and the bad come out but the good always comes out stronger, which is lovely if you're on your own, having strangers looking out for you.'

# THE SMALLEST ACT
## OF KINDNESS IS

## *worth more*

## THAN THE
## GREATEST INTENTION.

KAHLIL GIBRAN

# KINDNESS IS FREE TO GIVE BUT PRICELESS TO RECEIVE

# VIRAL KINDNESS

When Becky Wass from Falmouth felt helpless in the face of the coronavirus crisis, she found a simple way to help out. She was worried that members of the local community who were self-isolating might not have a way to collect shopping or run errands. And she knew that people who were living alone might experience loneliness. So Becky designed a small postcard that she would be able to put through her neighbours' doors. She used the card to introduce herself and list ways in which she could help, such as picking up shopping, posting mail, delivering urgent supplies or simply phoning them for a friendly chat. With the card, Becky's aim was to spread kindness, and she encouraged others to share the idea with the hashtag #viralkindness. She made the card template available for others to print, and communities all over the world have now been inspired to stay connected locally. 'I do think in times like this everybody wants to do something to help, and this postcard just makes that a little bit easier,' Becky said.

# Dolphin games

Dolphins in Queensland, Australia, started to miss human interaction so much that they began to bring 'gifts' for anyone who visited them. The clever mammals brought shells, wood and coral from the seabed and presented them to any human they saw. The owners of a local café gave the animals fish in return for their presents.

# OPEN-AIR GIGS

Those lucky enough to live near Martin Taylor, a world expert at solo jazz guitar, were treated to some unique lockdown gigs in his front garden. Neighbours pulled up tables and chairs, and poured themselves a cold drink while listening to his jazzy riffs. Martin described his gigs as 'an hour of fresh air, music and friendship'.

# FORCE FOR GOOD

During the lockdown, a seven-year-old *Star Wars* super-fan ran 26.2 miles and raised over £8,000 for the homeless charity Crisis. Henry Cleary, from Stoke Poges in Buckinghamshire, completed the marathon in just 4 hours and 39 minutes over nine days. Henry said: 'I knew it would be tough and one day when it was really hot I thought I couldn't keep going but people cheered me from their windows and doorsteps, and it gave me a boost. I never thought I could run two or three miles every day, but I just thought of Luke Skywalker running down the Death Star Trench and that I was helping homeless people, and it kept me going. It really made me feel happy and proud, and I really hope that other children can feel happy too when they are running, even if coronavirus is still going on.'

# A-lister lockdown

Hollywood star Matt Damon was in lockdown with the locals in a village in Ireland. The celebrity was regularly spotted doing his food shop at the local supermarket, SuperValu, and even used one of their plastic bags to carry his wet swimming stuff after a dip in the sea. The actor was filming in Dalkey when travel restrictions were put in place. As his family was already with him, he decided to stay and enjoy his time in Ireland.

# KINDNESS CAN'T BE QUARANTINED

WE CAN

*create*

HEALING BY

*learning*

HOW TO BE KIND.

LADY GAGA

# LOVE YOUR NEIGHBOUR

It's not many who could boast having a former *MasterChef* contestant deliver food to their door, but that is exactly the service that Anthony O'Shaughnessy provided for his elderly neighbour Peter during lockdown. Anthony whipped up delicious meals every day while he quarantined with his family in Newcastle at the house that once belonged to his late grandmother. Neighbour Peter used to look after Anthony's grandmother by mowing her lawn and getting her groceries, so Anthony was delighted to have the opportunity to repay his kindness. The *MasterChef* UK competitor, who made it to the 2018 semi-finals was working from home, testing out recipes. 'I told Peter that there's plenty to spare, I can just put some on a plate and put it on your doorstep and ring the doorbell,' said Anthony. He cooked up everything, from quiche to broccoli Parmesan farfalle pasta and meatball tagine.

# TOOT FOR JOY

A church community in New York organised a surprise for a teenage boy battling a brain tumour. As he was unable to have visitors and was feeling particularly isolated, his friends and other church members piled into cars in their hundreds and drove past his house, tooting their horns in a procession of friendship and connection.

# ARISE, SIR TOM

Second World War veteran Captain Tom Moore captivated the nation when he decided to raise £1,000 to celebrate his one-hundredth birthday. He started to walk laps of his garden with the aid of his walking frame to raise money for the NHS and soon word got out about his efforts. His fundraising skyrocketed, as donations hit the million mark and Captain Tom promised to keep going for as long as the money came pouring in. The charitable hero raised over £33 million for the NHS, was knighted for his efforts and inspired the nation to do good during the unprecedented coronavirus crisis. Captain Tom was sent more than 25,000 birthday cards to celebrate the milestone, meaning staff at the South Midlands Mail Centre had to reprogramme sorting machines to deliver his post into a dedicated collection box. He urged the nation to follow his example by caring for others. He said: 'As you go along, give everyone a little smile and see if you get a smile back. This is something that might do a lot of good.'

NO ACT OF KINDNESS, NO
MATTER HOW SMALL,

*is ever wasted.*

AESOP

# CONCLUSION

In this book are examples of acts of kindness, both grand and everyday, because no act of kindness is ever too small. The coronavirus crisis hit the world hard, with so many losing their lives. Fear can often cause people to be unkind, but it was kindness that won out. This book is a tribute to anyone who performed an act of kindness during the coronavirus crisis and reminds us to hold onto hope, even during times when it feels like there is none. Remember, if you can be anything, be kind.

If you're interested in finding out more about our books, find us on Facebook at **Summersdale Publishers** and follow us on Twitter at **@Summersdale**.

**www.summersdale.com**